To The Marxists:

Long Live Innovationism!

By Caleb T. Maupin

Center for Political Innovation

To The Marxists: Long Live Innovationism!

Caleb Maupin
Copyright © 2024 Caleb Maupin

CONTENTS

To The Marxists: Long Live Innovationism!

This text is being composed in the direct aftermath of the 2024 Presidential Elections, and what a strange political situation we find ourselves in. The bulk of the American people are tired of their living standards dropping amid inflation and are opposed to further involvement in foreign wars. They reject the political correctness imposed on them from above, as well as the censorship and control exercised by tech monopolies.

Kamala Harris promised more of the same, while Trump beat his chest in support of various anti-establishment and pro-growth sentiments, along with fearmongering about immigrants and social conservatism. Trump won by a landslide, and now the left, including the "Marxists," writhes in anger. We are in a bizarre political space where the very wars, censorship, austerity, and inflation that Trump's voters rallied against are labeled "communism" and "Marxism" by those who oppose it.

Rather than correcting them, this label is embraced by the bulk of the "socialist" and "Marxist" voices that have emerged over the last decade to dominate internet spaces, where the vast majority of these discussions are now had. They are proud contrarians, embracing the worst ideas ascribed to them by their right-wing opponents, beating their chests while shouting, "yes, but it's good!" They gleefully align with the State Department and mainstream media like CNN in defense of wars, political repression, censorship, and declining living standards. They embraces the notion of "degrowth" arguing we need to reduce consumption and the population as a moral necessity. They loudly celebrate the FBI or CIA's attacks on the freedom of Americans they disagree with. They provide cover for (and often actively applaud) the collaboration between social media companies and the state in actively censoring not only their opponent's opinions, but even those they ostensibly agree with! "Socialists" and "Marxists" in our time are not dissidents or people providing an alternative. In our current political landscape, "socialism" and "communism" is the one of the main masks warn by the imperialist camp and its most shrill defenders.

This text is part of a complete reinvention that the Center for Political Innovation is undergoing. We exist to win, and that means understanding that the world has changed in the last century and the urgent need to adapt. The urgent need of our time is a bloc of anti-imperialists within US society, mobilizing working people to assert their economic interests against the big monopolies. Our goal is a society where banks, factories, and industries are organized to serve the public good, not the profits of a wealthy few. We want to unleash human creativity and growth to new heights, create vast abundance, and eliminate poverty and scarcity entirely.

This book is composed as a message to the "Marxists," any of whom might bother to read it. It is written in their language as an answer to their concerns, primarily addressing why, despite our beliefs remaining the same, we no longer seek to occupy their spaces or claim a place in their discourse. We do not want to be "Communists" or "Marxists" anymore. Doing so would only hinder us from doing what urgently needs to be done. This may be hard to grasp at first, but this text will explain why, to those who care to learn.

The responses to this text and the preceding announcements are predictable. The first response from "Marxists," mainly a collection of internet fandoms, will be to (incorrectly) exclaim, "Aha! They admit it! We were right all along! They are not Marxists but secret Nazi-Rapist-Pedo-Laroucheists! We were right the whole time!"

People of such a mindset are worthless to engage with, and the majority of self-identified "Marxists" in our time are *just like them*. They want anyone they are not directly affiliated with to be "wrong" so their particular fandom can be "right." They don't want unity to defeat imperialism; they want to be entertained by their favorite internet personality and whatever "beef" they currently have. Regarding the Center for Political Innovation, what we are actually doing or what we truly believe is totally irrelevant to them. If we ever accomplish anything for a cause they claim to support or say anything they deem correct politically, it only makes them hate us even more, seeing us as competitors(!) rather than the traditional "fellow travelers."

Despite the fact that such people have no interest in listening, we will state what will be obvious by the time this pamphlet concludes to any honest readers: our beliefs have NOT changed. We still want to defeat imperialism. We are still in favor of a rationally organized economy to eliminate the irrationality of profits in command. We still stand in solidarity with those across the world resisting imperialism and with the vibrant new economy emerging around the world as a result of anti-colonial revolutions. To us, this is what being a Communist was always about. However, it is no longer about that for the overwhelming majority of communists in America. It is also no longer about that for the overwhelming majority of people who oppose the emerging low-wage police state and the march toward war.

There may be another layer of cynical/reactionary anti-communists who will read this text or see its existence in yet another negative light, saying, "So, Caleb and his band of followers have decided to pretend not to be communists to trick a bunch of Trumpers into joining their movement? What a dumb idea! Not falling for it, comrades!" Well, this is equally incorrect. We have fundamental differences with what calls itself "Communism" in the Western world and even with aspects of authentic Marxism-Leninism. We are not simply rebranding the Soviet ideology. The world has changed, and so has anti-imperialism globally. Anti-imperialist political forces in the United States should follow suit. Our differences make it clear that we should not associate with "communism" or contend for a spot within it. We need to build something new and different.

As will be explained below, we believe we are holding on to the revolutionary essence of Marxism-Leninism—the revolutionary essence that the "Communists" discarded long ago. Furthermore, we openly admit that certain aspects of the Marxist-Leninist worldview are fundamentally wrong, and we have broken with them. We have deviated in a number of ways, as has the majority of communist-led governments and anti-imperialist forces around the world. We gain nothing from pretending we are the "true" communists when the majority of the forces we support no longer make this claim.

It must be said that "self-id" is not automatically reflective of one's actual beliefs. One could call themselves "a fascist" and know next to nothing about what that actually means. To put forward a "no true Scotsman" argument about what "communism" really is (and who is a "real communist") only serves to create market segmentation in fandom-building (as will be discussed more later); creating in-groups and out-groups to argue with/about.

We want to put ourselves above these silly semantic games. Even if we could successfully "win" the argument and force our detractors to acknowledge we are "the real communists" or more authentic representatives of the legacy of Marxism-Leninism, what would be the point? Would this get us any closer to defeating imperialism or rescuing our country from the current crisis? Being "the real communists" is not what we aspire to be. We aspire to change the world, teach people and help others realize that they can change the world as well.

There is a great deal of nuance in this text. These concepts are very complex. This text has been written for those in the Center for Political Innovation who come from the Marxist tradition, and for those outside the organization who have a foundation in Marxism and are trying to understand where we are coming from. Honest readers will learn a lot, not just about our beliefs, but about our exciting project to build a truly revolutionary anti-imperialist movement in America. Read this text carefully. Don't be afraid to read a section several times to truly grasp the essence of what is being said. This text was intentionally written to be concise and to the point, so many key concepts have been densely packed into these paragraphs.

WHERE DO WE STAND?

A good rule to live by is: "Never say anything you do not know to be true, but if something is true, and you know it to be true, do not be afraid to scream it from the heavens." This is a tradition our organization strives to uphold and put into practice.

So, in light of this principle, what is true in our time? What understanding does the Center for Political Innovation hold onto and scream from the heavens despite the denials and obfuscations that surround us?

1. The Western imperialist financial system is in severe crisis and must be defeated. The system of production organized for profit, which has evolved into an apparatus of trusts, cartels, and syndicates based in Western countries, is the main barrier to human progress and increasing human happiness. It is the primary enemy of the people of the world, including the overwhelming majority of the American people. The big monopolies and bankers who dominate the world from Wall Street and London must be defeated. It is in the interests of all humanity, and almost all of the American people, for this outdated, irrational mode of production to be replaced by an economy that works in the interests of society as a whole, not just the profits of a wealthy few.

2. Central Planning Works. The myth of the 20th century, that "Communism failed" and "the Soviet Union never had any economic successes," is pure poppycock. The Soviet Union boomed in the 1930s with the Five-Year Economic Plans, rapidly industrializing without the chaos of the market. Many other countries followed suit, industrializing, eradicating illiteracy, and building modern infrastructure led by revolutionary anti-imperialist governments that mobilized the population and centralized the economy. The idea that free markets are the only way to create growth has been thoroughly disproven by basic economic data. The Soviet Union, China, and many other states with largely state-run economies have had overwhelming success in raising living standards and increasing GDP. Criticisms of human rights, consumer goods, or other issues in these societies are deflections from an obvious reality: the Western imperialist system is impoverishing countries across the developing world and currently causing a dramatic drop in living standards within the imperialist homeland. Meanwhile, countries that have broken away from this system and adopted an economy where profits are not in command have had astounding successes eradicating poverty, industrializing, modernizing and advancing human progress.

3. Modern technology necessitates moving beyond "profits in command."

Technological advancement should make life more comfortable and easy, but in the irrational system of production organized solely to maximize profit for private owners, it leads to economic chaos and frequent gluts on the market. The value crisis ("overproduction") and the falling rate of profit necessitate that a popular government control the economy to ensure continued growth as technology advances. The problem of poverty amid plenty—want created by abundance—becomes intensified with technological progress. The AI computer revolution has created a nearly permanent crisis in Western societies and necessitates a planned economy more than ever before. Hunger caused by an abundance of food, homelessness caused by an abundance of housing, labor becoming more efficient and productive resulting in lower wages and unemployment—all of this is irrational and unnecessary. The technological breakthroughs of recent years could become glorious blessings for the human race, rather than the apocalyptic curse they currently threaten to be. Society must seize control of the economy and rationally organize it so these irrational problems causing so much misery can be eliminated.

4. Eurasia is rising while the West falls; we must embrace multi-polarity for mutual growth. The new bloc of countries centered around Russia and China points to the future. A layer of governments that emerged as a result of the victories of anti-imperialism in the 20th century has laid the basis for a new axis in the global economy. These societies are not deteriorating as the West is, and the future of America lies in aligning with and trading with this new, emerging economy—not violently opposing it. A multi-polar world, where the United States and Europe are integrated into a system of cooperation with Eurasia, could lead to living standards for all humanity reaching greater heights than ever before. A new world beyond imperialism is the only way forward.

At some point, names and labels have to change. This is not merely a marketing decision or branding in the crass social media sense. Names change when the essence of one trend becomes so distinct from another that it is in the interest of all parties to change the term that refers to them. Reluctance to change can occur because this shift is usually preceded by a heated debate about what the essence of a previously existing trend actually is.

Let me point to two previous examples, which should be highly relevant to those following the Center for Political Innovation's work.

Bolsheviks opposed Social-Democracy

In 1917, Lenin returned to Russia after the toppling of the Czar during the February Revolution. In his well-known April Theses, officially titled *The Tasks of the Proletariat in the Present Revolution*, Lenin instructed the Bolsheviks to change their name. He included a critical footnote stating: "Instead of 'Social-Democracy,' whose official leaders throughout the world have betrayed socialism and deserted to the bourgeoisie (the 'defencists' and the vacillating 'Kautskyites'), we must call ourselves the Communist Party." Lenin urged his organization to adopt the label "Communist" rather than "Social Democrat" because their movement had long been at odds with mainstream Marxism.

In his numerous works, including *Imperialism and the Split in Socialism* and *Imperialism: The Highest Stage of Capitalism*, Lenin made it clear that the Social-Democratic Parties were his enemies. His movement aimed to align with national liberation movements in the colonized world against imperialism, rather than with pro-imperialist "socialists." Addressing the official "socialist" groups of Europe, he asserted that a victory of socialism would entail their defeat, writing that his movement "is moving and will move, is proceeding and will proceed, *against* you; it will be a victory *over* you."

Lenin saw himself as the true Marxist, the most sincere social democrat. He passionately argued that he was preserving the revolutionary essence of Marx's teachings against the distortions of reformists and sellouts. He pointed to Marx's writings on Ireland and Poland as proof that Marx was evolving in his understanding of anti-colonial struggles. Lenin further highlighted how Engels acknowledged sections of the British working class that benefited from colonial wealth.

While Lenin did indeed adhere to certain Marxist principles that others had abandoned, he was also developing new theories based on the changing global landscape. Lenin emphasized the need for a revolutionary working-class government—something the Second International was straying from. In addition to preserving the revolutionary aspects of Marxism's core, Lenin adapted them to his new theories, including his concepts of imperialism, nationalism, and the Party of a New Type.

Lenin's theory of imperialism, his teachings on nationalism, and his vision of a Party of a New Type were all innovations. He took from Marxism what the Second International had forsaken, which he considered, correctly, to be the revolutionary essence of Marxism. He then introduced a new understanding of the global economy, a novel model for political organization, and a new strategy for engaging with the peasantry and oppressed nationalities. In his address to the 2nd Congress of the Communist International, he outlined how Bolshevism had a new perspective on the global economy: "Imperialism's economic relations constitute the core of the entire international situation as it now exists. Throughout the twentieth century, this new, highest and final stage of capitalism has fully taken shape. Of course, we all know that the enormous dimensions that capital has reached are the most characteristic and essential feature of imperialism. The place of free competition has been taken by huge monopolies. An insignificant number of capitalists have, in some cases, been able to concentrate in their hands entire branches of industry; these have passed into the hands of combines, cartels, syndicates and trusts, not infrequently of an international nature. Thus, entire branches of industry, not only in single countries, but all over the world, have been taken over by monopolists in the field of finance, property rights, and partly of production. This has formed the basis for the unprecedented domination exercised by an insignificant number of very big banks, financial tycoons, financial magnates who have, in fact, transformed even the freest republics into financial monarchies."

In 1916, amidst the reformist parties' betrayal by supporting World War I, Lenin made it clear that the Second International was his enemy. His goal was not to recruit them but to oppose them and to rally the masses against them. He wrote:"Neither we nor anyone else can calculate precisely what portion of the proletariat is following and will follow the social-chauvinists and opportunists. This will be revealed only by the struggle, it will be definitely decided only by the socialist revolution. But we know for certain that the "defenders of the fatherland" in the imperialist war *represent* only a minority. And it is therefore our duty, if we wish to remain socialists to **go down *lower and deeper*, to the real masses**; this is the whole meaning and the whole purport of the struggle against opportunism. **By exposing the fact that the opportunists and social-chauvinists are in reality betraying and selling the interests of the masses**, that they are defending the temporary privileges of a minority of the workers, that they are the vehicles of bourgeois ideas and influences, that they are really allies and agents of the bourgeoisie, we teach the masses to appreciate their true political interests, to fight for socialism and for the revolution through all the long and painful vicissitudes of imperialist wars and imperialist armistices. The only Marxist line in the world labour movement is to explain to the masses the inevitability and necessity of breaking with opportunism, to educate them for revolution by waging a relentless struggle against opportunism, **to utilize the experience of the war to expose, not conceal, the utter vileness of national-liberal labour politics.**" (Emphasis C.M.)

By 1917, the Bolsheviks were not social democrats; they were Communists. In his speech to the 2nd Congress of the Communist International, Lenin argued that social democracy was an integral part of the imperialist system, not a confused or weakened opposition to it. He stated "Before the war, it was calculated that the three richest countries—Britain, France and Germany—got between eight and ten thousand million francs a year from the export of capital alone, apart from other sources. **It goes without saying that, out of this tidy sum, at least five hundred millions can be spent as a sop to the labour leaders and the labour aristocracy, i.e., on all sorts of bribes. The whole thing boils down to nothing but bribery.** It is done in a thousand different ways: by increasing cultural facilities in the largest centres, **by creating educational institutions, and by providing co-operative, trade union and parliamentary leaders with thousands of cushy jobs.** This is done wherever present-day civilised capitalist relations exist. It is these thousands of millions in super-profits that form the economic basis of opportunism in the working-class movement. **In America, Britain and France we see a far greater persistence of the opportunist leaders, of the upper crust of the working class, the labour aristocracy; they offer stronger resistance to the Communist movement**. That is why we must be prepared to find it harder for the European and American workers' parties to get rid of this disease than was the case in our country. We know that enormous successes have been achieved in the treatment of this disease since the Third International was formed, but we have not yet finished the job; the purging of the workers' parties, the revolutionary parties of the proletariat all over the world, of bourgeois influences, of the opportunists in their ranks, is very far from complete." (Emphasis C.M.)

Communists supported **national liberation struggles**, whereas social democrats did not. For instance, Stalin explained in his lectures entitled *The Foundations of Leninism* how the Bolsheviks supported a conservative monarchist, the Emir of Afghanistan against imperialism, while opposing European "Labour Parties" that, despite their names, served imperialism. Stalin explained: "The unquestionably revolutionary character of the vast majority of national movements is as relative and peculiar as is the possible revolutionary character of certain particular national movements. The revolutionary character of a national movement under the conditions of imperialist oppression does not necessarily presuppose the existence of proletarian elements in the movement, the existence of a revolutionary or a republican programme of the movement, the existence of a democratic basis of the movement. **The struggle that**

the Emir of Afghanistan is waging for the independence of Afghanistan is objectively a *revolutionary* struggle, despite the monarchist views of the Emir and his associates, for it weakens, disintegrates and undermines imperialism; whereas the struggle waged by such "desperate" democrats and "Socialists," "revolutionaries" and republicans as, for example, Kerensky and Tsereteli, Renaudel and Scheidemann, Chernov and Dan, Henderson and Clynes, during the imperialist war was a *reactionary* struggle, for its results was the embellishment, the strengthening, the victory, of imperialism. For the same reasons, **the struggle that the Egyptians merchants and bourgeois intellectuals are waging for the independence of Egypt is objectively a *revolutionary* struggle, despite the bourgeois origin and bourgeois title of the leaders of Egyptian national movement, despite the fact that they are opposed to socialism; whereas the struggle that the British "Labour" Government is waging to preserve Egypt's dependent position is for the same reason a *reactionary* struggle, despite the proletarian origin and the proletarian title of the members of the government, despite the fact that they are "for" socialism**. There is no need to mention the national movement in other, larger, colonial and dependent countries, such as India and China, every step of which along the road to liberation, even if it runs counter to the demands of formal democracy, is a steam-hammer blow at imperialism, i.e., is undoubtedly a *revolutionary* step." (Emphasis C.M.)

Communists believed capitalism had entered a new stage, while social democrats did not. They opposed World War I and sought to transform it into civil war, whereas social democrats supported the war effort, mobilizing labor unions in favor of imperialism. Social democrats maintained loosely democratic organizations that deteriorated into "debating societies," while the Bolsheviks preserved a highly disciplined organization with a unified political line.

If Marx had been alive in 1917, he might well have joined the Bolsheviks. However, by that year, the Bolsheviks were not social democrats; they were Communists. The name change was necessary because what had once been a single political movement had diverged into two distinct trends.

Christianity broke from Judaism

One finds a similar parallel in the history of Christianity. The movement that Jesus Christ created, led by his twelve disciples, considered itself to be a form of Judaism. Jesus was called a "rabbi." He taught in the Temple of Jerusalem and considered himself to be the rightful interpreter of the teachings of Abraham, Moses, and the other Hebrew prophets. He was believed to be the Messiah they had predicted. His movement was built on the foundations of a previous revival among Jews started by his cousin, John the Baptist.

During his lifetime, Jesus instructed his followers, "Do not go among the Gentiles or enter any town of the Samaritans. Go rather to the lost sheep of Israel" (Matthew 10:5-7). He made it clear that his mission in life was aimed at his fellow Jews, saying: "I am not sent but unto the lost sheep of the house of Israel" (Matthew 15:24).

The Jewish leaders, the Pharisees, and the Sanhedrin rejected Jesus' claim that he was the Messiah and collaborated with the Roman Empire to bring about his persecution, considering his movement to be apostasy. Jesus had many heated arguments with the Jewish leaders, saying to them: "If God were your Father, you would love me, for I have come here from God. I have not come on my own; God sent me. **Why is my language not clear to you? Because you are unable to hear what I say. You belong to your father, the devil, and you want to carry out your father's desires.** He was a murderer from the beginning, not holding to the truth, for there is no truth in him. When he lies, he speaks his native language, for he is a liar and the father of lies. **Yet because I tell the truth, you do not believe me!** Can any of you prove me guilty of sin? If I am telling the truth, why don't you believe me? Whoever belongs to God hears what God says. T**he reason you do not hear is that you do not belong to God**" (John 8:42-47).

Jesus went on to say that his teachings were more important than those of the Hebrew prophets: "Now we know that you are demon-possessed! Abraham died, and so did the prophets, yet you say that whoever obeys your word will never taste death. Are you greater than our father Abraham? He died, and so did the prophets. Who do you think you are?" Jesus replied, "If I glorify myself, my glory means nothing. My Father, whom you claim as your God, is the one who glorifies me. Though you do not know him, I know him. If I said I did not, I would be a liar like you, but I do know him and obey his word. **Your father Abraham rejoiced at the thought of seeing my day; he saw it and was glad.**" "You are not yet fifty years old," they said to him, "and you have seen Abraham!" **"Very truly I tell you," Jesus answered, "before Abraham was born, I am!"** (John 8:52-58). On this occasion, the Jewish leaders were so angered by his words that, as the Gospel of John says, they picked up stones to throw at him, and he had to hide himself to escape the temple.

While Judaism maintained very strict rules for observing the Sabbath Day, with extreme punishments for violating it, Jesus openly flaunted these rules. Once, after healing a man on the Sabbath and being confronted for doing so by religious leaders, he replied: "The Sabbath was made for man, not man for the Sabbath" (Mark 2:27).

The Ten Commandments were sacred in Jewish law, and once religious leaders hoped to trip up Jesus by asking him which of the Ten Commandments was the most important. He replied, "Love the Lord your God with all your heart and with all your soul and with all your mind. This is the first and greatest commandment. And the second is like it: 'Love your neighbor as yourself.' **All the Law and the Prophets hang on these two commandments**" (Matthew 22:35-40).

The Bible makes it clear that Jewish leaders were key in arranging for the Roman Empire to execute Jesus by crucifixion. After his resurrection, Jesus appeared to his disciples on the mountain in Galilee and told them, "All authority in heaven and on earth has been given to me. **Therefore go and make disciples of all nations**, baptizing them in the name of the Father and of the Son and of the Holy Spirit, and teaching them to obey everything I have commanded you. And surely **I am with you always, to the very end of the age**" (Matthew 28:16-20). At this point, it seems clear that Jesus was no longer instructing his followers to recruit among the "lost children of Israel" but among people of other nationalities.

After Jesus' death, the movement proliferated, still viewing itself as a form of Judaism, with Jewish leaders considering it to be a deviation or sect. One of the Jews who was primarily responsible for repressing early Christians was named Saul of Tarsus. Saul had a vision on the road to Damascus: "He fell to the ground and heard a voice say to him, 'Saul, Saul, why do you persecute me?'" (Acts 9:3). Saul then became "The Apostle Paul" or "St. Paul" and converted to the faith he had been persecuting. As the movement began to proliferate throughout the Roman Empire, it increasingly had to face the fact that it was very contrary to what the known world considered to be Judaism.

Jews had the Ten Commandments. Jesus had said the two greatest commandments were to love your neighbor as yourself and love your God, and that these two commandments were far more important than the Ten Commandments. Jews honored the Sabbath and adhered to strict regulations about observing it. Jesus openly flaunted these rules, declaring, "The Sabbath was made for man, not man for the Sabbath." Judaism was a tribal religion that one was born into, with conversion not emphasized, and Jews did not proselytize. Jesus instructed his followers to "make disciples of all nations."

As the church spread, the Apostle Paul declared that one of the most important aspects of the Jewish faith, and one of the biggest barriers to conversion, could be set aside: "A person is not a Jew who is one only outwardly, nor is circumcision merely outward and physical. No, a person is a Jew who is one inwardly; and **circumcision is circumcision of the heart, by the Spirit, not by the written code**. Such a person's praise is not from other people, but from God" (Romans 2:28-29).

When the Apostle Paul wrote about how one could be circumcised "by the spirit," rather than physically, he was essentially confessing that his movement was no longer Judaism. Christianity rightfully claimed to be from the lineage of Moses and Abraham, but it had become so different from what the world understood to be Judaism that it was in the interests of all parties for a new name to be given, especially as it was converting mainly non-Jews and had parted with the Sabbath, the Ten Commandments, circumcision, and almost all the key practices of the Jewish faith, while proclaiming Jesus to be superior to Abraham.

Christianity and Judaism were, at this point, distinct religions, even though Jesus insisted he was preserving the truths of the Hebrew prophets, which the contemporary Jewish leaders had betrayed. What the world knew as Judaism and what Christianity had become were two distinctly different religions. Thus, the name changed.

WE PRESERVE THE REVOLUTIONARY ESSENCE OF MARXISM-LENINISM

The moment where Bolshevism stopped being Social-Democracy and became Communism, the moment where the followers of Jesus stopped being Jews and became Christians, is the moment where the Center for Political Innovation sits in the United States. We rightfully claim the heritage of Marxism-Leninism. We preserve from Marxism-Leninism what we consider to be its revolutionary essence, and we condemn the various "Communists" of U.S. society as traitors to this legacy. Likewise, they condemn us with vile hatred and slander, often intended to pave the way for direct government persecution.

This is what we preserve from Marxism-Leninism, which they have abandoned:

1.   **Marxism-Leninism is anti-imperialist and says that the western imperialist system is the main impediment to growth and human progress, and that all anti-imperialist forces must be supported.** The various Communists in the United States twist the definition of "imperialism" to make Russia and China somehow imperialists. They repeat propaganda against the forces opposing imperialism. They condemn anti-war sentiments among the masses as "conspiracy theories." They speak in outdated pre-Leninist terms about industrial workers and factory owners, and condemn talk of "globalism" and "international bankers" as anti-Semitic. We preserve what Lenin spent his life proving, that capitalism had entered the monopolistic stage of imperialism, and that "socialism" that supports imperialism is worthless, while anti-colonial and anti-imperialist movements for national liberation must always be supported.

2. **Marxism-Leninism believes in economic growth and increasing the productive forces.** The higher stage of Communism, as envisioned by Marx, requires vast material abundance. In *Critique of the Gotha Program*, Marx explained: "**Right can never be higher than the economic structure of society and its cultural development conditioned thereby.** In a higher phase of communist society, after the enslaving subordination of the individual to the division of labor, and therewith also the antithesis between mental and physical labor, has vanished; **after labor has become not only a means of life but life's prime want**; after the productive forces have also increased with the all-around development of the individual, and **all the springs of co-operative wealth flow more abundantly** – only then can the narrow horizon of bourgeois right be crossed in its entirety and society inscribe on its banners: From each according to his ability, to each according to his needs!" (Emphasis C.M.)

Marx spent his life explaining how capitalism was unable to create sustainable long-term growth and has frequent gluts of overproduction, poverty created by abundance. Marx explained the nature of the value crisis and the tendency of the falling rate of profits, and socialism is a mechanism for unleashing the productive forces with rational planning of the economy. In the *Communist Manifesto*, Marx explains that the entire reason for the proletariat seizing and centralizing the means of production is: "to increase the total of productive forces as rapidly as possible."

These "Communists" promote degrowth and argue that capitalism's flaw is that it creates endless economic growth. They say this growth must be stopped in order to save the planet from climate change, and because wealth and money are somehow spiritually impure. The "communists" oppose economic growth and worship poverty. They fetishize destruction and repeat climate alarmism to justify austerity and the destruction of productive forces. They believe an egalitarian society can somehow be created in poverty, and that the expansion of productive forces is somehow contrary to the goal of moving toward the higher stage of communism.

3. Marxism-Leninism has no loyalty to 'The Left' of Imperialism. Lenin saw the social democrats as his enemies. While at times it might be strategic to align with them, as he explained in *Left-Wing Communism: An Infantile Disorder*, they would be supporting them 'as a rope supports a hanged man.' During the early 1930s, the Communist International directed its main efforts against social-democracy or "social fascists" who mobilized the labor movement against the Soviet Union. The 1929 Program of the Communist International, adopted after the Sixth World Congress, said: "The principal function of social democracy at the present time is to disrupt the essential militant unity of the proletariat in its struggle against imperialism. In splitting and disrupting the united front of the proletarian struggle against capital, social democracy serves as the mainstay of imperialism in the working class." During this period, Stalin courted various industrial capitalists to be allies of the Soviet Union in industrializing, and the Communist Parties focused on building independent labor unions controlled by Communists and mobilizing the unemployed. As Trotskyites and other anti-communists constantly point out, from 1928 to 1935, the Communists focused primarily on calling out and opposing forces on the left, namely, Social-Democracy, the "left" face of imperialism.

However, after the 1935 7th World Congress, the Communist International completely shifted its orientation, and Communists sought a strategic alliance with the Social Democrats against fascism. Georgi Dimitrov instructed the Communists of the world to seek unity with the social democrats and to actively prop up the "left" face of imperialism, in opposition to fascism, its "right" face, which was then the primary threat.

Dimitrov went as far as urging the Communists to force a United Front and prop up social democracy against fascism, even when the Social Democrats rejected their appeals for unity: "We do not regard the existence of a Social-Democratic government or of a government coalition with bourgeois parties as an insurmountable obstacle to establishing a united front with the Social-Democrats on certain issues. We believe that in such a case, too, a united front in defense of the vital interests of the working people and in the struggle against fascism is quite possible and necessary. It stands to reason that in countries where representatives of Social-Democratic parties take part in the government, the Social-Democratic leadership offers the strongest resistance to the proletarian united front. This is quite comprehensible. After all, they want to show the bourgeoisie that they, better and more skillfully than anyone else, can keep the discontented working masses under control and prevent them from falling under the influence of Communism. The fact, however, that Social-Democratic ministers are opposed to the proletarian united front can by no means justify a situation in which the Communists do nothing to establish a united front of the proletariat."

Both of these tactics were completely legitimate and correct, based on the circumstances. Sometimes the imperialist left may be the greatest enemy; at other times, it might be a strategic ally. This is based on the circumstances. Marxism-Leninism has no loyalty to the "left" of imperialism against the "right."

However, this is completely forgotten by the overwhelming majority of Communists in the West. They believe that the New Right (Trump, AFD, Brexit, Le Pen), who represent the lower levels of capital, at odds with the overall imperialist agenda of NATO and the European Union, are the greatest danger. This is objectively false, as this layer is less in favor of economic degrowth, less in favor of suppressing civil liberties, and less in favor of escalating toward war.

The belief in loyalty to "the left" at all times is based largely on anti-populism and ethnic/religious bigotry, as well as decades of trauma from political repression and violence going back to the Cold War. Regardless, this loyalty to "the left" and revulsion with "the right" is a complete departure from the revolutionary essence of Marxism-Leninism.

4. Marxism-Leninism seeks to create a planned economy. Marxism-Leninism seeks a society where the centers of economic power are centralized and rationally planned. Socialism is the abolition of the anarchy of production, the chaos of the market. The *Communist Manifesto* says: "The proletariat will use its political supremacy to wrest, by degrees, all capital from the bourgeoisie, **to centralize all instruments of production in the hands of the State**, i.e., of the proletariat organized as the ruling class; and to **increase the total of productive forces as rapidly as possible**." This first stage of a planned socialist economy struggling against imperialism is said to lay the basis for the vast expansion of production and abundance necessary to reach the ultimate goal of a stateless, classless world.

Engels described socialism as: "The difference is as that between the **destructive force of electricity in the lightning in the**

storm, **and electricity under command in the telegraph and the voltaic arc**; **the difference between a conflagration and fire working in the service of man.** With this recognition, at last, of the real nature of the productive forces of today, **the social anarchy of production gives place to a social regulation of production upon a definite plan,** according to the needs of the community and of each individual… The proletariat seizes political power and turns the means of production into State property."

Despite this being the most blatant and obvious principle of Marxism-Leninism, most "Communists" bearing Marx and Lenin's names and symbols do not advocate a centrally planned economy. In some cases, they advocate the violent overthrow of the government and its replacement with a regime committed to an agenda of social justice, anti-racism, feminism, etc. In some cases, they advocate only voluntary worker-cooperatives. In some cases, they advocate an expanded welfare state created by "taxing the rich" and "abolishing billionaires." In some cases, they advocate that the country be reduced to rubble and ruin as the "evil racist society" is punished while the "racist Euro settlers" atone for their crimes. In some cases they advocate that the United States be divided up among various Native

American tribes who be given full sovereignty to impose whatever economic and political system they want.

While all these new "communists" share the same libidinal satanic fetish for violence and destruction, and the same hatred and lust for revenge against the bulk of the population, none of them advocate the most basic goal of historical socialist movements, even predating Marx. The elimination of the anarchy of production, and the establishment of a socialist planned economy is not only something they do not advocate but something they actively oppose and call "fascist." How can we be part of a movement that does not even share the basic elementary goal with us?

So, why change our name: Because of these above 4 points, which are basic to Marxist-Leninist theory, put us completely at odds with 99% of those who call themselves "Communists" in the west. Furthermore, those within western countries who are the most receptive to understanding these points, and have the most to gain from mobilizing around them and defeating imperialism, are the ones who are the most rightly at odds with the "Communists" who violently oppose both them and us.

By (1) **opposing imperialism**, (2) **believing in economic growth**, (3) **rejecting an assumed loyalty to "the left" of imperialism**, and (4) **striving to build a rationally planned economy**, we preserve the revolutionary essence of Marxism-Leninism. Our relationship with forces like the Communist Party of Great Britain (Marxist-Leninist) and other Communist groups around the world is based on their adherence to these principles and refusal to give them up as almost all other forces bearing the name "communist" in the western world have done.

The overwhelming majority of those bearing the name of "Communism" "Socialism" or "Marxism" in the United States do not believe in these things, and furthermore, are violently opposed to them. Meanwhile, the bulk of people among the population who are (1) **opposing the system of imperialism and the big monopolies**, (2) are **in favor of economic growth and fighting against degrowth economics**, (3) **opposing the imperialist left** and (4) **would ultimately have their aspirations realized by a planned economy**, are correctly mobilizing to protect their communities from the "Communists" who oppose them.

If you oppose the overwhelming majority of the "communists" and they oppose you, if you are aligned with the majority of the population and layer of society who fights against these "communists," and you have nowhere near the control of the means of communication that these two contending groups have as they share a definition of "communism," rather than childishly screaming in isolation about semantics, a name change is necessitated.

The anti-imperialist movement to unleash humanity's creative potential must just recognize that it has entered a new stage. That stage is called Innovationism. The Center for Political Innovation is providing the new orientation for the fight ahead.

WHERE DO WE STRAY FROM MARXISM?

While we preserve the revolutionary essence of Marxism-Leninism, we must admit that we have strayed from some of its key teachings and principles. There is no reason to deny this or gloss over our beliefs, despite the fact that these changes will no doubt be disapproved of by the majority of Marxist-Leninists still willing to collaborate with us in our anti-imperialist mass work.

We have preserved the revolutionary essence of Marxism-Leninism, but we have strayed from much of its baggage and orthodoxies.

We do not promote Dialectical Materialism. The concept of dialectical materialism is the foundation of Marxist thought, but our approach at the Center for Political Innovation seeks to draw from a broader set of perspectives. Dialectical materialism is a framework built upon materialist philosophy and Hegelian dialectics. The school of thought views all material realities as constantly changing, with contradictions driving social and historical progress. While some of our members may personally align with aspects of this perspective, our organization's philosophy does not rest solely on this foundation. Our membership is diverse, encompassing Christians, Muslims, Jews, Pagans, hard materialists, and those with other beliefs.

For many of us, the motivation to engage in anti-imperialist work comes not just from material analysis but also from deeply emotional and spiritual connections. These feelings—whether rooted in a higher power or a profound sense of justice—have been central to our persistence and unity. Acknowledging this does not require a wholesale rejection of materialist or dialectical approaches; instead, it reflects our openness to multiple ways of understanding and engaging with the world.

It's also important to clarify what dialectics entails. Far from "promoting conflict," dialectics seeks to understand the contradictions inherent in material and social conditions. While such contradictions often lead to struggle, the framework itself does not advocate discord but aims to analyze the forces shaping historical change. The association of conflict with dialectical thinking often overshadows its more nuanced purpose, and it is worth disentangling this misconception.

That said, our organizational focus is not on amplifying division but on fostering reconciliation, unity, and collective action. The cultural trends of cancel culture and "call-out" politics, which dominate Western leftist discourse, do not align with our vision of a more cooperative and inclusive anti-imperialist movement. These tendencies may seem "dialectical" as they emphasize intense struggle between people, but they tend to serve an individualistic rather than scientific or ideological purpose. These competitive and personalistic tendencies often obscure material realities and hinder the building of solidarity necessary for meaningful change.

Instead of celebrating conflict and struggle as end unto itself, we look to historical examples of anti-imperialist victories such as the Communist Party of China's unification of diverse social forces to establish the People's Republic in October of 1949. In 1980, Deng Xiaoping described it this way "China always used to be described as 'a heap of loose sand.' But when our Party came to power and rallied the whole country around it, the disunity resulting from the partitioning of the country by various forces was brought to an end. So long as the Party exercises correct leadership, it can rally not only its whole membership but also the whole nation to accomplish any mighty undertaking."

Our practice reflects a recognition that conflict is sometimes necessary—imperialism cannot be confronted without struggle—but it is not the sole driver of societal progress. By cultivating a sense of oneness and spiritual peace, we aim to bridge the divisions within society and among those committed to anti-imperialism. This approach does not reject the insights of dialectical materialism or Marxist thought but expands upon them, integrating emotional, spiritual, and material motivations to meet the challenges of our time. We embrace a broader, more inclusive perspective that unites rather than divides. This nuanced orientation allows us to draw from the rich traditions of Marxism and spirituality alike while remaining firmly committed to our anti-imperialist mission.

We recognize Non-Marxist-Leninist Socialism. During the Cold War, a number of governments emerged that were rooted in anti-imperialism and adopted centrally planned economies, but were not led by Marxist-Leninist parties and had ideologies that diverged from Marxism-Leninism.

In Africa, Kwame Nkrumah modernized Ghana based on the principles of "African Socialism." Julius Nyerere led Tanzania under his interpretation of African Socialism called *Ujamaa*. In Egypt, military leader Gamal Abdel Nasser aligned with the Soviet Union and the Egyptian Communist Party, yet promoted his own ideology, "Arab Socialism." The Ba'ath Party, a split from the Syrian Communist Party which had opposed French colonialism during World War II, spread throughout the Arab world, eventually gaining power in Iraq and Syria. Moammar Gaddafi developed Libya through the principles of Islamic Socialism. The 1979 Islamic Revolution in Iran established a state-run economy managed by a network of Basij Councils, which they described as a "resistance economy," or "Not Capitalism, But Islam."

Since the fall of the USSR, Bolivarian Socialism has flourished in South and Central America. Venezuela's government has endured significant attacks and remains a solid outpost of socialism and anti-imperialism. The Sandinistas in Nicaragua, while influenced by Marxism-Leninism, define their anti-imperialist, state-run economy under the banner of "Christianity, Socialism, and Solidarity."

These governments arose in part because Marxism-Leninism had become a "brand" associated with political organizations rooted in the Communist International. In these anti-imperialist revolutions, where creating a planned economy was necessary to liberate nations from imperialist domination, a party other than the Soviet-aligned Communist Party often took power. However, despite differences in ideology, the economic policies of these parties were largely similar to those of Marxist-Leninist parties: they seized control of key sectors of the economy and mobilized the population to industrialize, aiming to build a planned economy free from imperialist control.

The reasons for these non-Marxist-Leninist parties taking the lead are complex and tied to the unique circumstances of each country. In Iran, for instance, the Communist Tudeh Party had collaborated with imperialists, while secular Soviet-aligned Iraq became the primary antagonist to the revolution, cementing the role of Ayatollah Khomeini and his Islamic Revolutionary Party. In Iraq and

Syria, the Ba'ath Parties often presented a bolder revolutionary program and were less hostile to Islam than the official communist parties, which often functioned as diplomatic lobbies for the Soviet Union and took a more reformist stance. In Latin America, official communist parties sat at the center of broad united fronts against neoliberalism and austerity, and in Venezuela, the Communists largely merged into the United Socialist Party. In Libya, Egypt, and Ghana, the revolutions emerged from military factions that admired the Soviet Union and held anti-imperialist beliefs. Members of the official Communist parties in these countries would not have been allowed to enter the high ranks of the military before the anti-colonial revolutions, and would not have had the influence necessary to lead the military in an anti-imperialist direction. While these countries had socialist revolutions and established anti-imperialist states, they did not do so with the Marxist-Leninist ideology.

Marxist-Leninist governments still exist in China, Cuba, North Korea, Vietnam, and Laos. Additionally, there are governments that began as Marxist-Leninist states but have since become ideologically eclectic. The governments of Angola, Namibia, Eritrea, and Mozambique were founded by Marxist-Leninist parties that have since shifted to self-identify as "social democratic" since the 1990s. The Zimbabwe African National Union - Patriotic Front (ZANU-PF), founded by Robert Mugabe, was originally a Marxist-Leninist party and it never repudiated the ideology. It now governs Zimbabwe and its ideology is unclear. Alexander Lukashenko, President of Belarus, took office during the collapse of the Soviet Union and preserved much of the Soviet economic structure. While he has referred to himself as a Communist and has recently praised Marxist-Leninist ideology, his rhetoric is quite eclectic.

There are likely other examples of governments, current or former, that fit this category. However, the key point is that socialism—defined as an anti-imperialist state with a planned economy—exists beyond Marxist-Leninism and the Soviet model. Even Marxist-Leninist governments have become ideologically diverse in recent years. Official Communist Party publications defending "Socialism with Chinese Characteristics" have incorporated elements of Confucianism and quoted the work of Nietzsche, thinkers who are not aligned with Marxist principles, alongside the work of Mao Zedong and the classical Marxist writers. Similarly, Cuban government media displays ideological eclecticism, while North Korea maintains that its *Juche* ideology transcends Marxism-Leninism, even though it was originally based on Marxist-Leninist principles.

This reality underscores the absurdity of the idea that only governments with explicitly Marxist-Leninist ruling parties can be considered socialist. The Soviet Union itself did not adhere strictly to this belief, referring to countries such as Iraq and Libya as "Socialist-Oriented Governments." The first book published by the Center for Political Innovation was *The Green Book* by Gaddafi, which was released to affirm Libya's status as a socialist state and to criticize the lack of solidarity with Libya during the 2011 Civil War.

In the West, the majority of Communists have broken with all existing socialist and anti-imperialist states, labeling them as "Stalinist," "State Capitalist," or "Revisionist." A small minority of Western Communists still support China, Vietnam, Cuba, North Korea, and Laos, but they often try to separate these states from others like Venezuela, Nicaragua, Iran, Syria, and Zimbabwe, claiming some ideological "class line" divides them. We argue that no such line exists, and inventing one for the sake of ideological consistency is misguided. Claims that Iraq had a "national democratic revolution" with the working class central to the regime, while Cuba underwent a "full socialist revolution" are unfounded and desperate attempts to impose a narrative on reality. Gaddafi's Libya that, applied to join the Warsaw Pact, was not a "bourgeois national regime" while China with its huge market sector is a "workers state." This is just nonsensical thinking.

There is no magical class divide between anti-imperialist states. The only way an anti-imperialist state can build an economy independent from imperialism (as Iran's Supreme Leader calls it, a "resistance economy") is through asserting state control and planning. Without this, free competition would allow imperialist monopolies to dominate.

During the Cold War, various pro-imperialist regimes, often authoritarian and bonapartist in nature, were propped up by the West, utilizing military power to stabilize their economies. Most of these regimes (such as those of Marcos, Pinochet, Park Chung-Hee and Noriega) were phased out in the 1990s by Western "human rights" forces led by George Soros, as the threat of communism had diminished. A few regimes, such as Saudi Arabia and Singapore, have maintained authoritarian structures with heavy state control of the economy but operate profit-based economies, maximizing profits for private owners. These are still profit-centered economies, despite massive state control. The state facilitates the flow of money into the hands of the ruling families. Saudi Arabia's royal family uses its massive profits to stabilize the economy through military spending and redistribution among relatives. Singapore's economy is controlled by four ruling families, who maintain their dominance through the military, and stabilize the economy to some degree while making sure it functions to maximize their profits.

While some regimes, such as the Burmese military junta, promoted their own "road to socialism," they remained profit-oriented economies. By contrast, Iraq, Libya, Syria, Iran, Venezuela, Nicaragua, and other anti-imperialist states have built economies that are not driven by profit maximization but by state control, backed by a well-organized population. These countries have integrated heavily with the Soviet Union and are now part of the emerging BRICS-led sector, showing a fundamentally different economic character from those of imperialist-aligned states.

The market has a role in socialism. During the early years of the Soviet Union, the country had a completely militarized economy—"war communism"—to defeat the White Army and foreign invaders. Then Lenin launched the New Economic Policy and reintroduced the market in order to stimulate the economy. Later, Stalin mobilized the population to build up heavy industry with Five-Year Economic Plans, and agriculture was collectivized in response to a food crisis and counter-revolutionary mobilizations by the Kulaks.

By the 1960s, it became clear that while the Soviet economy was very effective in producing steel, managing natural resources, and providing education and basic infrastructure, it had limitations in the area of consumer goods and services. A layer of counter-revolutionaries, who eventually toppled the USSR, was recruited from the frustrated intelligentsia who often felt stifled within a completely state-run economy.

After the death of Mao Zedong, Deng Xiaoping won many of the alienated intelligentsia back to supporting the party by introducing market reforms. China's astounding economic growth came with state control over the economy but allowed foreign investment and a market sector.

The governments of Iraq, Iran, Libya, and modern-day Russia and Venezuela maintain a model that might be called "Petro-Socialism," where the state controls key natural resources and utilizes the revenue from these resources to stimulate and plan a mostly private economy reliant on energy revenue.

In Nicaragua, the socialist economy has had its greatest successes with the micro-entrepreneurship program. Like Venezuela, worker-owned cooperatives for-profit enterprises complement a largely state-directed and subsidized economy.

The lessons of the 20th century and the proliferation of socialism and anti-imperialism into the 21st century have made it pretty clear that the market has its place. Profits should not be commanded. The economy must be controlled by a powerful, revolutionary state rooted in a well-organized population that has defeated the imperialists. But within such a model, a market can provide for the things that make life enjoyable: hotels, restaurants, clothing, children's toys, entertainment, computer software, etc. Having individuals invent and innovate new ideas, and letting consumers vote with their dollars to some degree on what is best, doesn't weaken the socialist nature of the economy.

Socialism is not about making everyone equal. Lenin and Marx both made this very clear. Lenin went as far as saying: "The first phase of communism, therefore, cannot yet provide justice and equality; differences, and unjust differences, in wealth will still persist." Marx made clear that the basis of the even playing field in a higher phase of communism, along with the withering away of the state, is vast abundance, not a forced or engineered equality from above (firmly *rejecting* equality on a legal basis!)

Pol Pot's "Democratic Kampuchea," China's Cultural Revolution, Che Guevara's failed experiments with "New Socialist Man" in the early years of the Cuban Revolution—all show that forced equality in conditions of scarcity is a recipe for disaster. The entire point of a socialist state or "dictatorship of the proletariat" is to centralize the instruments of production in order to raise productive forces. The socialist state eliminates the problem of overproduction and the chaos of the market and unleashes growth, propelling humanity toward the level of technological abundance that can create the higher state of communism.

Forced equality and redistribution of income, rather than rational planning of production, have nothing to do with socialism. Every Marxist-Leninist government in the world recognizes this. But Communists in the west do not. They often maintain China and Vietnam's current economic setup is "revisionism." Borrowing from liberals, they condemn "inequality" in income in socialist societies. From this point, we strongly diverge from "Communists" in the west, and are fully in line with the existing communist governments, who admit they have to some degree deviated from the political line or Lenin and Stalin.

We Do Not Practice Democratic Centralism - In 1903, Lenin proposed his "Party of the New Type" as an effective model for utilizing the strength of all of Russia's greatest revolutionary organizers. The idea was that in a highly disciplined organization of professional revolutionaries who give "the whole of their lives," the strengths of many brilliant thinkers, agitators, and organizers could be combined to make a powerful revolutionary organization capable of actually taking power.

Democratic Centralism means that all members of the party are obligated to carry out all its decisions and adhere to its line, regardless of their own feelings. Democratic Centralism means debate is kept internal. Democratic Centralism means that rather than having a private press or individual expression, official party organs whose leadership is politically assigned function as the way the parties ideas are communicated after the line has been wrangled over internally.

The Democratic Centralist method was very successful in the Bolshevik revolution, but even during these times its was apparently much looser than Lenin would have preferred. Central Committee members Bukharin and Zinoviev famously opposed the planned seizure of power by the Bolsheviks and announced it to the capitalist press in September of 1917. Lenin was overruled by the rest of the Central Committee when he demanded they be expelled for something that would have resulted in execution in most military situations.

After the Russian Revolution, Trotsky, as foreign minister, refused to sign the Treaty of Brest-Litovsk and prolonged Russia's involvement in the First World War. Though the party had sent him to sign the treaty, with his own line on "Permanent Revolution," he did the exact opposite of what the party told him to do and yet remained a key player in Soviet politics for over another half-decade.

Democratic Centralism was a very effective attempt to unify revolutionaries to march as one. However, in the United States and modern Western countries, in an age where information flows much more freely and conditions do not necessitate revolutionary activity, Democratic Centralism has been a recipe for failure. In battlefield conditions, where survival means marching as one, the minority may submit to the majority in the name of preserving an organization that is necessary for survival and to ensure victory. However, in less urgent conditions, a minority that doesn't get its way simply walks away to form a new organization.

Social-Democratic and Communist organizing methods were always designed to be labor union-adjacent. Social-Democrats and Marxists were people involved in labor unions who had a particular political ideology. They organized people in a single workplace or neighborhood out of unified economic interest to struggle against their employers. The Bolshevik organizing methods, along with the previous social-democratic methods, worked well in these contexts.

However, in our time, when activism becomes more a matter of personal indulgence—proving how smart you are or how moral you are for taking a stand—the need to form a unified organization evaporates. Democratic Centralism demands that every member of the organization repeat a single line. Democratic Centralism demands rigid control over published materials and activism. The various attempts to form Democratic Centralist organizations in America are walking examples of why such methods are not successful.

Democratic Centralism has come to mean the exact opposite of what it meant for Russian Marxists in the 1900s. Instead of bringing many revolutionaries together to combine their strength, it has come to mean each "vanguard party" must be dominated by a single "big brain" or "big giant head." With a loyal group of members, this leader gets his way on every issue and establishes "the line." Those who disagree are outvoted and forced to go along with it. If they disagree or even continue to "open a closed discussion," they are expelled. Eventually, those who do not become part of the Big Giant Head's fandom, and who want more input into what the organization does or more free expression in their revolutionary propaganda work, walk away.

During the 1930s, there were three major Marxist tendencies in America: the Socialist Party, representing Social-Democracy; the Communist Party, representing Marxism-Leninism; and the Trotskyites, representing their deviant anti-communist pseudo-Bolshevism. All three groups had major thinkers, intellectuals, labor leaders, and mass organizers among their ranks. They fought with each other and disagreed, but they remained in the same organization. Those organizations had hundreds of thousands of members who saw the organization as essential in building the labor movement and asserting their economic needs.

Post-WW2, each party has gradually devolved into an intellectual fandom centered around one person, or one small group. People join them to carry out activism they feel morally compelled to do, and to learn about and proselytize what is considered to be an obscure and forbidden ideology in the United States. These parties have big difficulties holding on to members and simply do not sink their roots into the masses of people. The demand that people intellectually conform and obey in conditions that do not necessitate that creates a situation where the "big giant head" has no reason to compromise with weaker factions, and dissidents have no reason to stay in an organization where they'll be constantly overruled. The demand that entire group adhere to a single line makes division inevitable.

In more recent times, the new generation of "big brains" haven't bothered to start parties. They simply start YouTube channels or social media followings. Their followers don't do activism; they simply consume the messages and hover in Discord servers.

What the United States needs at this time is not another "democratic centralist" vanguard party, and attempting to set one up would lead to further political ineffectiveness. The Center for Political Innovation is struggling each day to figure out how to build an anti-imperialist bloc within U.S. society. Adopting some imitation of Bolshevik methods of rigidity would not help us in this process. Being involved in our day-to-day activities makes that clear.

We Do Not Claim Comintern Lineage – Some of our members were once in the Communist Party USA. Others were in the Party for Socialism and Liberation, the Party of Communists USA, Workers World Party, Progressive Labor Party, or some other group. However, we claim none of their groups as heritage, and we do not fit our ideology or worldview into a political family tree.

The necessity of being a split from a split from a split, tracing your heritage back to Marx himself, is one of the greatest stupidities of Marxist politics. Serious political parties do not claim such heritage. This kind of identity is the basis for building obscure sects. This is where Marxism takes on the characteristics of a religion rather than an effective political movement.

The Center for Political Innovation seeks to engage in "political innovation." If a great discovery about how to effectively organize is made by some other trend, we would seek to learn from it and adopt it as we can. We do not pretend that if Marx were alive today, he would join our ranks, because that is irrelevant. The issue at hand for our organization is how effectively we can build an anti-imperialist movement.

HOW DO WE RELATE TO OTHER ANTI-IMPERIALISTS IN THE UNITED STATES?

There is a layer of Americans who support the new economy that is rising around the world and oppose the decaying imperialist system. It is a small percentage of the U.S. population, but it is rapidly growing as instability increases and the realities of the changing character of the global economy become more obvious. This layer of Americans tends to also oppose economic degrowth and the attacks on our civil liberties.

Unfortunately, most of these Americans are not politically active but merely consume alternative media. The majority of them are not Marxists or Communists but have a "conspiratorial" perspective, heavily influenced by Libertarianism and the more anti-establishment side of the 1960s New Left. A significant layer of Communists does exist in these circles, and a wider layer of people influenced by Communist ideas or previous experience in communist organizations exists among them.

Various writers and internet personalities like Jimmy Dore, Kim Iverson, Max Blumenthal, Oliver Stone, Ben Norton, Abby Martin, Scott Ritter, Alex Jones, and Garland Nixon are popular among this anti-imperialist layer of Americans. They tend to watch RT, PressTV, Telesur, and other media from anti-imperialist countries, as well as content from various YouTube channels and podcasts. Some may participate in protests supporting the Palestinians or against police brutality. They joined the Rage Against The War Machine protests in Washington, D.C., in February of 2023. Most are not politically activated but are just consuming alternative media.

There are some distinct ideological trends among the more active currents of this group. The anti-imperialist current is very diverse and certainly not the mainstream of either "the left" or "the right." It is worth understanding who these forces are, what they represent, and why we Innovationists may cooperate with them at times but represent a distinct political current of our own. Our goal is not to be king-makers or stage-managers of these circles, but to recruit normal working-class Americans who are angry about the conditions of declining imperialism and looking for answers.

We Are Not Marcyites

The overwhelming majority of American "communists" are not anti-imperialist. The Communist Party USA ran an article on its website claiming that Russia was a bigger threat to Europe than NATO and launched a hysterical witch-hunt against the Center for Political Innovation, obsessing over Alexander Dugin. In 2022, the various Trotskyite groups marched with Ukrainian flags taking their political lead from CNN. "Socialist" Kshama Sawant, a member of Trotskyite sect Socialist Alternative and former member of the Seattle City Council worked with the Democrat labor union bureaucrats to organize hostile protests against Chinese President Xi Jinping when he visited the United States.

While there may be mild sympathy for Cuba or Venezuela, spaces like the Left Forum, outlets like *Jacobin*, and organizations like the Democratic Socialists of America are pro-imperialist. They demonize Russia and China, sponsor and highlight US government-backed "dissidents" around the world, and provide a standard interpretation of global events that aligns with the US State Department's talking points.

Among the small minority of American communists who maintain anti-imperialist politics to some degree, the overwhelming majority come from an ideological current called Marcyism. Marcyism originated as an outlier pro-Soviet interpretation of Trotskyism, founded by Sam Marcy and the Global Class War Tendency. The group operated within the Socialist Workers Party of Buffalo, New York, during the aftermath of the Second World War. The Marcyites broke away from the Fourth International and Trotskyism in the late 1950s, eventually founding the Workers World Party.

Marcyites tend to believe they are the true inheritors of Trotsky's legacy but view the Trotskyist movement as counter-revolutionary. They often seek relationships with Marxist-Leninist and anti-imperialist governments around the world. They also tend to align with anti-revisionist Marxist-Leninist groups and the official Comintern-born parties of various countries. Sam Marcy led the Workers World Party in the late 1970s to transition to a strategy of leading large anti-war protests in Washington, DC, functioning as "movement managers" who dominated anti-war and leftist activist spaces by reserving permits and battling for control of coalitions.

Sam Marcy died in 1998, and the tendency has since fractured. The lineage and tradition of Marcyism today continues through the

Party for Socialism and Liberation (PSL), founded in 2004 and led by Brian Becker. Two other breakaways from Workers World Party, Struggle/La Lucha and the Communist Workers League of Detroit were both founded in 2017. In addition there are the Virginia Defenders and the New Orleans Workers Group, among a few other renegade sects and local activist collectives with Marcyite roots.

The Party for Socialism and Liberation has several hundred members and receives funding from pro-China billionaire Roy Singham, allowing it to operate impressive offices and pay a field staff of a few dozen organizers. Break Through News, Abby Martin, and Ben Norton function as social media mouthpieces for PSL's brand of late-Marcyism, while various other personalities throughout alternative media take ideological guidance and geopolitical orientation from PSL.

The other breakaway sects, including the remaining incarnation of the Workers World Party, have roughly 30 members at most and function as informal activist clubs that print newspapers, read each other's articles, and squabble at liberal protests and events supporting the Cuban government.

The essence of Marcyism is more in its practice than its beliefs. Marcyist groups support all forces around the world resisting imperialism and practice a form of "protest hustling," fundraising to stage liberal rallies and traveling to anti-imperialist countries in peace delegations. Marcyism has been thoroughly infiltrated by US intelligence agencies, and some of the smaller sects do little more than serve that purpose. The details on this are both tragic and comical at times. At the start of Russia's special military operation, the leader of one small sect wore a Russian military helmet in Donbass, embedded with the army, before running back to the United States to lead Black Lives Matter protests. Another leader formed the so-called "Odessa Solidarity Committee" and claimed to care about the people of the Donetsk People's Republic, positioning himself as a pro-Russia solidarity advocate. Yet, during the 2024 election cycle, he hysterically claimed that Trump's victory— which the Donbass people hoped would lead to a peace treaty—would result in "concentration camps."

The Marcyite strategy consists of staging rallies around trendy liberal causes, fetishizing the Black community, and constructing a kind of anti-imperialist counter-gang that functions as the voice of anti-imperialism within "the left." It sees US society as evil, imperialist, and doomed. It seeks to absorb misfits and alienated youth into a "new family" where they can help organize rallies, fundraise, and view themselves as the persecuted and righteous few.

In more recent times, Marcyite groups have become infected with Trump Derangement Syndrome, believing that by echoing liberal denunciations of Trump in the most shrill way possible, they can prove their revolutionary prowess. The *Workers World* newspaper carried the headline "Abortion on Demand for All Genders" in response to the Supreme Court overturning *Roe v. Wade*. The Communist Workers League of Detroit compared prosecuting Donald Trump to Lincoln disenfranchising Confederate soldiers. The internal life of these groups is a constant mess of cancel culture, accusations of racism and sexism, sexual scandals, mental health episodes among woke college students, crying, yelling, and accusations of fascism—all typical of woke spaces. If the entire scheme did not generate so much money for the Becker family or serve intelligence purposes for embedded US government informants, the current would likely have completely imploded.

The Marcyite approach was originally shaped in the 1970s. Marcyism's strategy is better understood if you watch films like *Network* (1976) or *The Spook Who Sat by the Door* (1973) and get a flavor for the political landscape of these times. This was the era when Angela Davis, a Black revolutionary, was the primary pro-Soviet public face, and various Third World Marxist-Leninist guerrilla forces had aesthetic ties to the "movement" of post-1960s radicals. During these years Gaddaffi was funding the Black Panthers, radical college students were flocking to Cuba by the thousands and adventurist groups like the Symbionese Liberation Army and Weather Underground were romanticized by a layer of anti-establishment youth.

Today, politics is completely different. In our time, Marcyism is shedding its anti-imperialist roots as it clings to "the left," with a practice that insists on positioning itself within the "left" side of imperialism. Marcy himself, a Ukrainian born immigrant who could remember the 1930s, had a much more populist and coherent understanding of Marxism methods and economic theories than his followers, mostly boomers plucked out of "the movement." Marcyite groups tend to pride themselves on how non-ideological and disinterested they are in history and theory. "We are the only group that actually does anything," each Marcyite sect insists.

Is the historical success of Marcyism before its current deterioration an influence on the work of the Center for Political Innovation? Of course. Marcyism's history of bold anti-imperialism in its ascendant period is admirable. Its solidarity with victims of state repression in the United States is important. However, the overall practice of Marcyism deviates from the revolutionary essence of Marxism-Leninism, as it seeks to be part of "the left." Marcyism's aspirations are extremely low, aiming to be nothing more than a symbolic counter-gang of anti-imperialists in US society. Regardless of Marcy's intentions decades ago, the Marcyites of our time have no real ambition to build a base among the masses. They view US society and culture, as well as the bulk of the population, with contempt.

We have certainly studied the practice of Marcyism. We seek to establish relationships with all anti-imperialist forces, engage in demonstrations and street activism, and create a community or family of activists for anti-imperialist operations.In this sense, we share some commonality with Marcyism and retain elements of its practice and beliefs.

But beyond these surface-level aspects, we stand in solid opposition to much of Sam Marcy's teachings. We do not seek to attach anti-imperialist forces around the world to the US "left." We reject a race fetish and white savior complex, though our solidarity with the Uhuru Movement in the face of political repression has been much stronger than that of almost all other anti-imperialist groups. We are not opposed to patriotism or cultivating a sense of national unity among Americans who oppose imperialism.

Our street demonstrations are often small and intended to be theatrical and attention-grabbing, unlike Marcy's strategy of broad left regroupings with themselves as stage managers. The activist community we build focuses on cultivating the creativity and innovation of each member, rather than demanding that the rank and file glorify the leadership. Ultimately, we aim to build a base among the general population, not a counter-gang of misfits or a fandom of an older activist guru.

Marcyism played a positive role in the 1970s and 80s but had its limits even then. Today, Marcyism is deteriorating, increasingly losing influence within anti-imperialist circles. It is also on the verge of shedding its anti-imperialism altogether, though this will take time. Over the past decade, imperialists have flooded social media with "Communist" voices who are pro-imperialist and aligned with the "left" side of imperialism. This will probably gradually crowd out the Marcyite remnants, leaving them with less reason to exist and eventually leading to their liquidation into the broader, pro-imperialist "left."

We are not Larouche-ists

Another trend that is highly present and visible in anti-imperialist circles today is Larouche-ism. The Marxist teacher in New York City known as "Lyn Marcus," who later reverted to his birth name "Lyndon Larouche," was the first to observe that US leftism was embracing "degrowth" and "Malthusian" economics, becoming a vehicle for the ultra-rich old money to control the lower levels of capital. Larouche saw that Marxism was pro-growth and loudly condemned how money from wealthy Anglo-Americans and Zionists was turning it into a form of pessimistic middle-class radicalism. Larouche believed that the New Left was reminiscent of 1930s fascism in its economic form and much of its spiritual content, and as a Trotskyite intellectual and self-taught economist, he mobilized against it. His National Caucus of Labor Committees battled the Communist Party and all the prevailing forces of American "communism" who were attached to the New Left and demanded it be tailed.

Larouche eventually renounced Marxism entirely and began promoting the economic theories of Friedrich List and Henry Charles Carey. He also became very hostile to a number of anti-imperialist movements and maintained the suspicion and hostility toward the USSR that he inherited from his Trotskyite days. However, he did embrace Baathism in the Arab world. In the early 1990s, a Larouche-ist split from the Communist Party of Ukraine called the Popular Socialist Party was formed, and the Chinese government developed a deep relationship with Larouche's organization during the 1980s and 90s that continues up to today.

At the same time, Larouche increasingly embraced various US-backed Bonapartist regimes as they were oriented toward infrastructure development, and he cultivated his cadre of activists to do intelligence work and activism in alliance with Ronald Reagan, Park Chung-hee, and various figures within the imperialist camp during the Cold War.

Larouche-ism openly seeks an alliance with some in the ruling class and the US state in order to advance their pro-growth agenda.

This level of honesty is something Leftist groups will loudly denounce, pointing to it as proof they are "fascists" and "government agents." The Leftists do this as if they are not obviously controlled and tied to intelligence. What Larouche admits and understands as a necessary part of maneuvering within US society, the Leftists do either as useful idiots or conscious liars.

Larouche-ism celebrates human creativity and, at this point, is sympathetic to Russia and China as a pro-growth axis against the decaying Western imperialist financial order. Larouche-ism has backed into becoming anti-imperialist, reluctantly, but this is not an essential part of its beliefs. The group carries a critique of "British Empire Economics" as opposed to the American System, but in practice, this has largely translated into supporting US-backed Bonapartists against "Communists" around the world.

In our time, because Larouche-ism is pro-growth and the "degrowth" trend among the imperialists now has dominance, Larouche-ism's primary entity, The Schiller Institute, now functions as a prominent anti-imperialist, pro-China, and pro-Russia voice. PrometheanPAC, previously known as LarouchePAC, broke with the Schiller Institute in 2020, and is hostile to China, more thoroughly embedded in Donald Trump's movement.

Larouche-ism is ideologically weak. It does not provide the basic economic understanding that imperialism's stalling of development is rooted in monopolism and the desire to maximize profits. Instead, Larouche-ism blames imperialism and degrowth on the "oligarchical conception of mankind." According to this view, imperialism results from bad ideas. If only the leaders of the US government listened to classical music and studied Larouche's favorite poets, they would enact humane and progressive policies. The Larouche movement sees itself as the inheritors of Plato and Socrates in a philosophical war against Aristotle that has raged for thousands of years among the elite. The cadre are mobilized to campaign for Diane Sare and other Larouche candidates, disrupt town hall meetings, and hand out leaflets as they entertain themselves by reading Shakespeare together and singing classical choral music in between.

The Larouche-ite current is wracked with paranoia and anti-communism. The rhetoric often focuses on conspiracy theories that are detached from any deeper analysis or understanding. For example, Marx was supposedly a British agent because he studied at a museum in London, and the poet

Shelley was assassinated by his wife, with Mary Shelley's novel *Frankenstein* allegedly being a coded attack on Benjamin Franklin and the American Revolution due to the use of lightning. Larouche insists various figures throughout history were British agents or assassinated rather than dying of natural causes, without a shred of evidence. Larouche-ists will assert these absurd, unproven claims as true without any evidence, mixing them with a lot of well-documented but not widely acknowledged truths in their various lengthy dossiers and publications. At the same time, they repeat standard anti-communist talking points about a system that "never worked anywhere" because "everyone gets paid the same wage," pandering to the lowest levels of anti-communist ignorance.

Overall, Larouche-ism, like Marcyism, has its limits and does not have the potential to become a mass movement or really build a base among the masses. Like Marcyism, it seeks to cultivate an activist fringe. While we give credit to Larouche for identifying the important divide in the ruling class as being growth vs. degrowth, we cannot claim the many bizarre twists and turns the organization has taken over the years as our own heritage. Larouche-ism, incarnated by the Schiller Institute, LarouchePAC/

PrometheanPAC, Webster Tarpley's Tax Wall Street Party, and a few other breakaway sects and deviations, is a distinct trend completely separate from Innovationism.

Do we draw from Larouche-ism? Well, we make a point of including music at our events. We see the "growth vs. degrowth" divide and the accompanying mindset as the primary division in the ruling class. We seek to cultivate a pro-growth mindset among our members and insist on constant optimism. We encourage members to examine their subconscious motivations and draw from the psychoanalytic tradition to enable themselves to be better activists. We do not seek to recruit from "the left" but from the masses overall. We view the bulk of the socialist and communist groups as controlled and utilized by imperialism, something Larouche was ahead of his time in calling out. We loudly condemn Malthusianism, just as Marx did. We also propose various infrastructure projects and trade corridors as realistic programmatic demands to advance anti-imperialism.

But beyond these points of overlap, our movement is quite non-Larouchian. We refrain from calling people British agents. We have a basic economic understanding of imperialism as monopolistic capitalism, not a result of an oligarchical mindset or degenerate aesthetics. We do not regulate the lives or media consumption of our members. We do not engage in intelligence work. We do not condemn rock music. We don't claim a lineage to Plato or Socrates except in a broad sense of the march of history and historical progress. We try to avoid paranoia and build broad alliances with all anti-imperialists who will work with us. While we may draw from Larouche-ism in some aspects of our thought and practice, we are not Larouche-ists.

We would be happy to cooperate with Larouche-ist entities at some point, as we did previously, as we share a great deal in terms of the main concerns that need to be addressed in our time. We share many allies with them, and it would make sense for any organizational tensions to eventually be overcome.

Internet Fandoms

Among the large number of young Americans who have begun identifying as Communists in the past 10 years, the primary way this ideology has proliferated has been through internet fandoms. The main leftist internet trend was called BreadTube. We revealed that BreadTube was an intelligence operation with a widely read book called *BreadTube Serves Imperialism.* Our work was later validated by investigative work from Grayzone. After the rise of Bernie Sanders it became necessary to prevent the new wave of young "socialists" from becoming anti-imperialists. U.S. and British intelligence agencies boosted a wave of "socialist" and "anarchist" internet personalities to build their own followings and carry out this operation.

In response to our efforts exposing BreadTube and pioneering anti-woke, anti-imperialist sentiment among internet socialists, a couple of new fandoms have emerged, promoting their own version of anti-imperialist, non-woke Marxism-Leninism. In total, there are fewer than 300 adherents of this obscure wing of "Communism" in the entire country who have ever attended a single in-person event, though they may have a wider internet audience of a few thousand.

Some voices within these circles are sincere in their beliefs but are extremely competitive and unfamiliar with how coalitions are built or operations conducted. Other voices are clearly plants by intelligence agencies, as they fail to grasp basic tenets of Marxist thought. They repeatedly show a lack of understanding of the Leninist definition of imperialism or other foundational concepts, and often inject anti-communist historical myths—like Bolsheviks "killing millions of

Christians"—into their attempts to mimic talking points from anti-imperialist media.

These individuals have no concept of building anything beyond a social media following, despite attempts to form an organization. Their circles consist of a few prominent social media influencers and a layer of bottom feeders who aspire to be big influencers themselves, hoping some clout will rub off on them.

For a time, some of these influencers were friendly toward the Center for Political Innovation. However, the entire time, they were merely taking notes, thinking, "How can we copy this in a way that lets us be in charge and exclude CPI?" A real organization requires allies, unity, and most importantly, real operations carried out by a trusted network of people. These factions envied the "glory" of CPI's accomplishments, like staging large events and attending international gatherings. However, beyond their envious, competitive mindset, they lack any vision of their own. Building a real organization and executing genuine operations are things they neither know how to do nor aspire to achieve.

They have no idea what a genuine mass anti-imperialist movement in America would look like. They only saw the beginnings of what CPI has done and were given every opportunity to cooperate with us. Instead of doing so, they exclaimed, "No! That should be ours!" The level of political immaturity from this collection of 20-year-olds—each of whom imagines themselves as the next Stalin—is astounding. They engage in social media cancel culture and harassment campaigns in the same way the woke-left does, only substituting terms like "white supremacist" and "fascist" with juvenile insults like "faggot." They lace their commentary on international events with pick-up artist dating advice and boasts about sexual conquests and exercise routines.

Despite raking in millions of dollars in social media revenue, these groups have not dispatched a single member to a Uhuru court date or demonstration, showing how surprisingly unconcerned they are about the criminalization of anti-imperialist speech. This further suggests that at least some of their top figures are likely law enforcement plants.

These fandoms see CPI as an enemy not because they want to strengthen anti-imperialism, but because they want to be kings of the internet, similar to how PSL wants to dominate the protest space. If people are reading our books, attending our events, or interacting with us in any way, they are not consuming content from these social media influencers. Thus, we become competition for their internet-based consumption operation.

Despite our efforts to maintain good relationships, they have been relentless in their childishness, competitiveness, and desire to keep a rivalry alive. Why? Because social media thrives on drama, scandal, gossip, and rivalry. If we were collaborating and doing the real work that needs to be done, they wouldn't generate much revenue or get many clicks or likes.

Part of the reason it is necessary to pivot away from the term "Communism" is that as long as we hold onto it, we will remain— or at least appear to be—a competitor or variant of what these clowns are trying to do. Our competition with them inadvertently helps guide them in figuring out how to solidify and prolong their embarrassing, counterproductive existence as loud voices supposedly representing anti-imperialism and "Communism." The further we can pivot away from appearing as if we are on a similar mission as these fools, the better.

We care about the Uhuru 3. They don't. We want to get real operations done and build a real organization; they want to fling insults across social media like deranged monkeys. They seek clicks and likes, while we aim to build a base among the population. Our criticism of them sustains them, so it must be completely silenced. Let them self-destruct with their juvenile rivalries and the same competitive spirit that drove them to attack us so viciously. Just like with the Synthetic Left, if these idiots are what the masses perceive as "Communism," we must rebrand ourselves as something entirely different in their eyes to accomplish our goals.

Libertarians & The Old Right

What is a "Libertarian?" In 2008, it was this appealing new ideology for college-aged non-conformists. "I'm socially liberal and fiscally conservative" was a phrase often uttered by many people trying to sound intelligent. "Ron Paul is the only good man in Congress" was another favored saying among suburban children of Republicans who were ready to rebel but shared their parents' contempt for Obamania.

On a personal note, as a college student, I could not stand Libertarians. I was frustrated because it seemed they had a mental block, refusing to entertain Marxist or Socialist ideas. They questioned mainstream media yet accepted shallow anti-communist tropes prevalent in U.S. society, assuming, "well, things are now bad, so that means America must be communist." My frustration with

Libertarians quickly turned to frustration with Marxist groups because they showed no interest in debunking Libertarian claims about economics. Many people I encountered in college and in life were making economic arguments I vehemently disagreed with, arguments that could be debunked with basic data. Yet, the Marxist groups were more focused on "building the movement," which, at that time, meant creating "street heat" to support Obama.

Fast forward a decade, when my social media began to gain traction, and as the internet left started targeting me with smears, one criticism I frequently received was "he argues like a Libertarian" or "he sounds like a Libertarian." I was perplexed by this, but essentially, the criticism meant, "he's arguing for creating economic growth" and "he's focusing on economic policies to improve people's lives." Even though I was advocating the exact opposite of Libertarian positions—calling for state control of banking and natural resources, and a popular government to oversee a rise in living standards—I still "sounded like a Libertarian" simply because I focused on economics.

Being labeled as "just like a Libertarian" was part of my realization of how far gone and spiritually bankrupt the left had become. Leftism was no longer about arguing that socialism was a better economic system that could deliver better results for the population. Instead, it was about denouncing people as "bad" for being racist, sexist, or homophobic. Leftism had become a vehicle for stoking resentment, manipulating trauma, fomenting jealousy, and certainly not about providing solutions. Although my positions were the opposite of Libertarian ones, I was still called a "fascist" because my motivation was similar: to create economic growth and improve people's lives. The left not only does not share this goal, but it is also fundamentally opposed to those who do. In our age, woke-ism and leftism have devolved into the psychology of pessimism, resentment, victimhood, virtue signaling, shame, guilt, vengeance, rage, and every other negative emotion, all packaged as an ideology. Leftism opposes not only certain economic principles or policies but also confidence, optimism, community, loyalty, and everything associated with happy, healthy people and a peaceful, prosperous society.

Alexander Dugin, the Russian philosopher popular in anti-imperialist countries, coined the concept of the "Fourth Political Theory." In his groundbreaking book published in the early 21st century, he argued that Liberal Democracy, the first political theory, was once again in crisis. The first attempt to defeat it, Communism, the second political theory, had failed. The second attempt, Fascism—the Third Political Theory or "Third Way"—had also failed. Dugin argued that Bolivarianism, the Shia Axis of Resistance in the Middle East, and the rise of Russian President Vladimir Putin signified the emergence of a "Fourth Political Theory" that combined elements of Fascism and Communism, the left and the right. The essence of this theory, according to Dugin, was a rejection of individualism and an embrace of collectivism. Western societies promote an ideology that prioritizes the individual above all else, while anti-imperialist states, no longer predominantly Marxist-Leninist, embrace a form of collectivism in opposition. One criticism of Dugin's analysis commonly leveled by Marxists is that he seems to take fascist rhetoric at face value, assuming that the words of far rightists in Europe represented their true aspirations and principles. Dugin's work presents fascism as a specific political theory and quotes its ideologues, rather than seeing it as a symptom of imperialist decay with ideology invented to justify the needs of the ruling elite.

On the surface, Libertarianism appears to be the antithesis of the Fourth Political Theory—

a full embrace of individualism, rejecting all forms of collectivism from both the left and right. Libertarians advocate for market liberalism and minimal government involvement in managing the economy. They also reject social conservatism, believing everyone should be free to live their life as they choose, with no obligations to community, country, or family beyond a vague social contract to respect others' property rights.

If taken at face value, Libertarianism should be our greatest enemy. However, as those familiar with Marxism and historical materialism understand, nothing is merely surface-level. The Protestant Reformation and ensuing wars across Europe were not just about theological differences, nor was the rise of fascism in the 1930s merely due to bad ideas gaining attention.

Dissident political trends in capitalist countries often represent economic strata at odds with the ruling class. Our own movement—Marxism and Social Democracy —emerged from the labor movement and the industrial working class. In the lead-up to World War I, Social Democracy split between sections of the labor movement (the 'aristocracy of labor') that aligned with imperialists and those opposing imperialism based on their economic interests.

So, what does Libertarianism represent? It's not hard to see that much of Libertarianism is a repackaged version of the "Old Right" that existed before Neoconservatism rose among Republicans in the 1960s and '70s. Ron Paul, the Republican Congressman most associated with Libertarianism, openly acknowledges his ties to the John Birch Society. He entered politics in Texas as part of the far-right resistance to the national shift away from McCarthyism.

The John Birch Society's founding text, *The Blue Book*, reflects how "far-right" politics was already changing at the time. Before World War II, the "far-right" did not advocate for free market policies; they embraced various fascist theories to crush communism while organizing the economy with significant state involvement.

After World War II, as the economy began booming again, industrialists who had been attracted to fascism saw their profits rise and shifted towards advocating for unregulated free markets. This was the direction the John Birch Society took, advocating for a "constitutional republic" with minimal state interference. However, *The Blue Book* still quoted Oswald Spengler and referenced pre-war right-wing thinkers who embraced forms of right anti-capitalism.

The Libertarian Party emerged in the 1970s, with an element of the Old Right seeking to combine its emphasis on personal liberty with the aspirations of counter culture elements that emerged from the New Left. While some more traditional old right elements like the Constitution Party and the American Independence Party stuck around, Libertarianism was a new brand. During the 1980s, the Koch Brothers and others within the Reagan camp utilized the Libertarian Party to give voice to their own values which clashed with neoconservatism. Symbolic election campaigns served as an opportunity to present a contrary ideology that appealed to different sentiments among the left and right.

Fast forward to 2008, after the financial crisis, and suddenly almost all Republican voices were "Libertarians." The neoconservative strategy of appealing to a silent middle-class white majority against non-conformist intellectuals and supposedly ever-complaining poor and minority groups was no longer effective. People losing their homes and jobs were looking for solutions, and Libertarianism offered an easy answer: "We just need to return to real capitalism."

Libertarianism became an ideology of austerity: if only all government workers were laid off, minimum wages abolished, and the economy completely deregulated, there would be endless prosperity. The economic problems, according to this new Republican line, were due to the U.S. being a "socialist" or crony capitalist economy. Mitt Romney's 2012 Presidential campaign that talked about cutting funding for PBS and emphasized his role as a businessman very much represented the peak of this new "libertarian" repackaging of a still largely neoconservative GOP.

The rise of Donald Trump shifted the Republican Party away from this performative Libertarian turn. Trump appealed to a sense of collectivism, condemning the rich and powerful, and presenting himself as a strongman who would use his power to change things, not just "get the government out of the way."

The Libertarian Party now faces an identity crisis. Some "Never Trump" Republicans who viewed Trumpism as a threat to their individualism have joined its ranks, while many traditional old-right elements have left for the Republican Party, finding a home in Trumpism. There is a layer of Libertarians tied to the tech world who are staunchly opposed to the U.S. imperialist state and its monopolies, even embracing Russian and Chinese perspectives on geopolitics, supporting Julian Assange, and opposing COVID lockdowns.

The Mises Caucus of the Libertarian Party appears to have gained control over the organization in the past few years, though its grip is far from secure. What seems to define the Mises Caucus is its sympathy for Russia and China, as well as its soft alignment with Trumpism. Trump addressed the Libertarian Party in 2024 and seems to have a cordial relationship with Angela McArdle, the Party chair. With the Mises Caucus in command, the Libertarian Party sponsored two anti-war rallies and a more ideologically driven anti-establishment rally in Washington, D.C. Instead of being an electoral entity that garners 2% in national elections, the Libertarian Party is now led by elements that see its influence growing as a more ideological part of the Trump coalition. In some ways, one could compare their strategy to how the Communist Party positioned itself during the late 1930s under Earl Browder's leadership, acting as an ideological and well-energized activist faction within Roosevelt's alliance.

At the end of the day, the lower-level capitalists who made up the old right, along with the tech millionaires who align with the Mises Caucus of the Libertarian Party, ultimately want to make money. It is the ultra-rich—what Carroll Quigley labeled the "Anglo-American Establishment"—who seek forced de-growth to stabilize the economy. The World Economic Forum and the financial maneuvers of BlackRock represent the schemes of this managerial ultra-rich. The old "Yankee and Cowboy War" between the managerial ultra-rich and the entrepreneurial majority of the capitalist class is hotter than ever. If lower-level capitalists want growth, the only way to achieve it is to break the power of the big monopolies. Lower-level capitalists are flourishing in the socialist countries of the world, and this is something many Libertarians acknowledge, even if it doesn't align with their ideology.

These lower-level, pro-growth capitalists will reluctantly come to understand that deregulation alone will not defeat the monopolies; instead, they will need a government that punches up. This realization will push them into an alliance with working families, laying the groundwork for the anti-monopoly coalition that the Communist Party proposed in the 1950s. In our time, the focus is on defeating the imperialists. The Libertarian Party, based on the economic interests of those aligned with it, is fighting against the imperialists. Anti-imperialist governments around the world draw their strength from an alliance with this very stratum, and an anti-imperialist government in the United States would as well.

It's worth noting the rise of Javier Milei in Argentina. Milei is anything but an anti-imperialist. His policies have centered on economic austerity and blatant alignment with U.S. imperialism on the global stage. However, he used Libertarian rhetoric to get elected, which appealed to a large segment of Argentine young men. In the modern "gig economy," many workers are technically "independent contractors" or small business owners. The laws are written in a way that treats them as if they are wealthy capitalists. These young gig economy workers do not identify with the labor movement and view labor unions as part of a rigid bureaucracy that enables state oppression.

The Communist and Social-Democratic movements have largely disappeared because they were always intended to be adjacent to the labor union movement. They have been replaced by the "New Left," mobilized by big capital to push for de-growth and regime-change "human rights" wars. A new kind of organization capable of winning over gig economy workers and addressing their interests as they struggle daily to pay their bills needs to be developed. The mindset of a gig economy worker—hustling through the day, unsure of how much cash he will bring home—is very different from the mindset of an industrial worker on the shop floor. Gig economy workers value their creativity and individual effort, often relying on these qualities to get by.

The ideological phenomenon of libertarianism further highlights why we can no longer be "Communists." Libertarianism, while incorrect and largely based on the delusion that capitalism can revert from its current stage of decaying imperialism back to its industrial era, is driven by an underlying opposition to the increasingly authoritarian society in which freedom is restricted to enforce de-growth, impoverishment, and depopulation. These are the same sentiments Trump tapped into to win the 2024 election. These are also the sentiments upon which a genuine anti-imperialist movement in this country will be built. Only a popular government backed up by a mass movement of the people can defeat the big imperialist monopolies. Only rational control over the economy can point the way toward the endless growth libertarians long for. The strata currently supporting the Libertarian movement will eventually be forced to recognize that it will need to align itself with a broad mass movement seeking a government of action that fights for working families.

WHAT IS OUR PRACTICE?

"Philosophers have only analyzed the world, the point however, is to change it."
- Karl Marx

It is time to just do it. None of the ideas floating around the various books, podcasts, livestreams, will mean anything if action is not taken. The situation is urgent.

Since 2015, there is a joke I have told to explain my frustration with "Communists." I will compose an updated version of it here, because the point still stands, and it explains why we cannot be "Communists" anymore pretty concretely.

The joke goes like this:

A wealthy New York City lawyer had an intense dream one night. In the dream, he heard the voice of God command him: "You must hire a Communist to work at your law firm!"

The man awoke from his dream in a frightened state, believing he had received a direct order from Almighty God. So, he immediately advertised that he wanted to hire a Communist to work in his law office.

He first hired an activist who was a member of the Communist Party USA. He took his new employee to a room with many important legal papers in it and instructed him to file the papers and organize them so they could be properly assessed. He told the elderly Communist Party USA national committee member that he would return at the end of the day to check on his progress.

When the lawyer came back at the end of the day, the papers were just as he had left them. The man had sat in the office and had not done a single bit of work, not filed a single paper. The lawyer said to him in frustration, "Why didn't you file the papers?"

The old Communist shot back, "Don't you see that Republicans control a big chunk of Congress, and Trump has just been re-elected? Now is not the time to file papers. We've got to defeat the ultra-right. Maybe, if Trump is impeached and driven from office and replaced with a Democrat, and Democrats control both houses of Congress, at that point, maybe we can start filing the papers. But until then, it's just out of the question."

The lawyer had never heard a more ridiculous explanation in his life. He fired the man and decided he must not be a real Communist. So, he went down to Greenwich Village and found a Trotskyite and a Maoist and immediately hired them. These are real Communists, he thought. They can get the job done.

He gave them the same instructions. When he returned at the end of the day, he found the office empty, with some of the legal papers missing. In a panic, he began looking for his lost employees.

He found the two college-aged radicals from rival Maoist and Trotskyite sects on the street corner in front of his office. They were standing there holding his legal papers, pestering various pedestrians walking by, attempting to sell them for one dollar.

He stopped them immediately. "What are you doing?" he asked.

"We're selling the papers! Like we always do," one man said.

"I told you to file the papers, not sell them!" the lawyer said, aghast at yet another idiocy from a Communist he had hired. He fired the two student Communists and set out to find yet another Communist to get the job done.

Next, he hired a well-known Communist social media influencer who wanted to make some extra cash. He gave him the same assignment. When he returned to the room of legal papers at the end of the day, he found that, yet again, the papers had not been filed. However, the young social media personality was live-streaming on his iphone.

"I just got a job at this based law firm filing papers!" he said into his phone's camera, while flexing his muscles. "I bet CumDumpster1917 wouldn't even get invited for a job interview! He's an idiot. And don't worry, I have not sold out! When I interviewed for the job, I made

sure they only hired Black Hispanic Transgender people and refused to represent law enforcement or anyone who makes more than $40,000 a year."

The lawyer was once again shocked, not just because the papers remained unfiled, but also because he had no such policy and primarily represented very wealthy corporate clients. He abruptly ordered the young aspiring influencer to end his livestream and fired him.

The lawyer decided to make one last attempt at hiring a Communist to file his papers. He hired a member of the Party for Socialism and Liberation (PSL). He took him to the room where the papers were stored and gave him the same assignment: to file the papers. When he returned at the end of the day, the room was empty and the papers were unfiled. However, on the desk, he saw a leaflet. The leaflet said, "Rally in Times Square to File the Papers" and gave a time and location. In utter shock and disappointment, the lawyer made his way to Times Square.

There, he saw a crowd of 50-60 people with protest signs, loudly chanting, "FILE THE PAPERS! FILE THE PAPERS!"

The lawyer couldn't believe his eyes. Soon, various speakers got up before the crowd and shouted into a bullhorn. A Palestinian speaker got up and said, "The fight to file the papers is also the fight for Palestine!" The crowd of smiling faces, hinting at fake enthusiasm, burst into a smatter of forced applause. The next speaker, a transgender sex worker, got up. "The fight of Transgender people is the fight to file the papers!" The crowd applauded once again with the same fake enthusiasm. "The biggest enemy of filing the papers is Donald Trump!" said one young activist into a bullhorn, "I just saw on MSNBC that he tweeted something racist the other day! He's a total Nazi!" The crowd began chanting "Fuck Trump! File the Papers! Fuck Trump! File the papers!"

The lawyer ran up to the young PSL member he had hired, who bore a very proud grin on their face, thinking they had far exceeded their new boss's expectations.

"What is wrong with you Communists? I have hired four different kinds, but not a single one of you can do the simple task of filing the papers," he said.

The PSL member's face fell, surprised at the lawyer's disapproval.

"How dare you compare us to those other groups!" she said. "The other Communists just talked about filing the papers! But we are the only ones who actually did something!"

There's a job that needs to be done. In this humorous parable, filing the papers is a stand-in for building an anti-imperialist movement among the American people. In short, the reason we must stop being "Communists" is because Communists are not doing this job, and further association with them will render us just as incapable of doing the job as they are.

To borrow from Mao Zedong's theory of protracted people's war and apply it to very different conditions, there are three modes of struggle that revolutionary organizations take on.

Strategic Defensive - This is the phase in which the revolutionary organization is isolated from the masses. The conditions are not at the point where the masses are sympathetic to the message or goal. The divisions in the ruling class have not intensified enough to enable the alliances needed that allow revolutionary organizations to flourish. The revolutionary organization struggles to stay intact, swimming against the current, and often fracturing as the benefits of unity are not apparent.

Strategic Equilibrium - This is where the game changes. The conditions among the masses have reached a point where they urgently need change and are ready to join organizations that can deliver both immediate relief and a vision of dramatic reinvention of society. The ruling class is fighting among themselves enough that revolutionary organizations can flourish in alliance with different factions, set up "turf" in specific areas, and become highly influential, mobilizing layers of the population for political action.

Strategic Offensive - As the crisis intensifies, one big dividing question faces society. The revolutionary organization has built up enough strength to represent the primary fighting force on one side of the polarizing question. As society clashes over the division, they mobilize one side of the question and ride this wave into taking power.

U.S. revolutionaries and anti-imperialists have been floundering in the strategic defensive phase since the 1950s. There was a moment during the late 1960s and 1970s when it seemed strategic equilibrium was imminent, but it ultimately did not emerge. The urgent necessity of the moment is to prepare for strategic equilibrium. Networks need to be created. Activists need to learn to cooperate and carry out operations together. We need to be preparing for the moment when we will be able to flourish. The rhetoric must be refined to have mass appeal, not an intellectual niche one. Buildings need to be acquired, and plans for acquiring "turf" across the country need to be laid out.

None of the various variations and deviations of Communism in America even aspire to build an anti-imperialist movement among the U.S. working class. They actively oppose doing it and are lined up with the ruling class to prevent it from happening. As the masses are awakening, growing more and more angry about their conditions, the "Communists" have mostly become defenders of the very things they are ready to fight against.

Communism has so long been an epithet and enemy in American society that its aesthetics have become a magnet for deviant individuals: angry teenagers rebelling against their parents, misfits who hate the society they live in, young men with Oedipal dictator fantasies, etc. None of this is the basis for a genuine revolutionary movement.

The red flag, the guillotine, the desire to unleash suppressed impulses—this was all the psychology that the bourgeoisie fomented to destroy the feudal order. While Communism attached itself to these aesthetics, the imperialists have now found them to be useful in spreading instability across the planet. The aesthetics of rebellion, depression, and vengeance belong to the imperialists at this point. They have become part of their color revolution apparatus. Meanwhile, anti-imperialist states often present a much more conservative message, offering protection from the chaos of the market and presenting the nation as a kind of family where all have a place and are cared for.

While the dying order screams "rebel!", a successful anti-imperialist movement based on the real economic needs of the population will most likely have a message of care, solidarity, and duty rather than the traditional mindset of leftist rebellion.

In this context, we cannot be Communists. We are forced to re-examine what Marx and Engels acknowledged to be the unique brilliance of humanity: our ability to reinvent our relationship with nature and propel ourselves to higher modes of production, higher social systems, a higher population, a longer life expectancy, and a better state of being. We take from Marxism its brilliant understanding of why technological development negates capitalism. We take from Leninism its brilliant understanding of imperialism and the struggle for national liberation. We look with inspiration to the various countries that have broken free from imperialism and organized their economies without profits in command to eradicate poverty and unleash expansion with 5-year plans. We seek to build such an anti-imperialist pro-growth government in our own country, actively building a movement intended to see that come into being as imperialism cannibalizes itself within its once prosperous homeland.

Communism or Marxism-Leninism was one stage of anti-imperialism. It had its great victories and laid the foundation for what exists in the world today. But we are not seeking to recreate the past, and we are not "Generals Fighting The Last War" trying to get right what previous entities got wrong.

We are pioneering new terrain. We are carrying out operations to promote anti-imperialism, and we are building and solidifying a network of people with which to carry them out. See the appendix, a timeline of our activities from the years 2023 and 2024 to learn what we are doing. If you get involved, you will learn about our very big plans for 2025 and beyond. With our limited resources and membership, we have accomplished the work of an army.

Our "communist" rivals and detractors do not notice what we have done, and they do not even understand the importance of this work. They are in a completely different category than us. They do not even aspire to do what we do. We must be clear with our words that we represent a completely different movement, with different goals, different beliefs, and a different orientation. We are not doing our own version of what the various "communists" are doing. We are doing something completely new so we can win in a completely new time with new conditions.

The low-wage police state and the danger of a new world war have not vanished simply because Trump won the election. The next four years will be an uphill battle full of setbacks, victories, and stalemates. New opportunities now exist for us to push anti-imperialism forward and build the needed anti-monopoly coalition, with the aim of breaking America free from imperialism and bringing into being a government of action that fights for working families. To remain "Communists" is to keep fooling around, not doing what we have set out to do.

Innovationism is a new stage, and we are ready to swing further into action. No looking back.

Goodbye, Communists. You want us to be your enemy, and at this point, we welcome your hatred. We have far too much important work to do, and we are far too aware of our deep responsibility in these crucial times to continue worrying about you or existing within your paradigm. We must move on to something higher.

LONG LIVE INNOVATIONISM!

2024 Timeline of CPI Activities

- **January 7th** - CPI called for a National Day of Action to oppose the bombing of Yemen. Protests were held in Portland, Humboldt, Chicago, and New York.
- **January 26th** - CPI published the book *Who Are the Houthis? What Are They Fighting For?*, detailing the history of the Ansar Allah movement and its struggle against imperialism and Zionism.
- **February 12th** - The books *Russia Is Not Our Enemy* and *Journey of Hope: Building a Movement for Peaceful Reunification of the Korean Peninsula* were published for distribution at the World Youth Festival.

- **February 15th** - The Center for Political Innovation was featured at an official United Nations press conference about the World Youth Festival. At the press conference, CPI highlighted the Uhuru case, expressed support for North Korea, discussed the upcoming trip to Russia, and answered questions from the UN press corps.
- **February 29th - March 7th** - CPI led and participated in the U.S. delegation to the World Youth Festival in Sochi, Russia. Three members attended, and two members spoke directly with Putin on the last day during a special session.
- **March 15th - 17th** - CPI members served as official observers of the Russian presidential election.
- **April 20th** - CPI published a new textbook titled *Out of the Movement, to the Masses! Anti-Imperialist Organizing in America*.
- **April 26th - 29th** - Thirty people attended a CPI workshop in Vermont titled "Out of the Movement! To the Masses!"
- **May 26th** - CPI distributed 1,000 copies of a new pamphlet called *Do You Believe in Growth?* at the Libertarian Party National Convention in Washington, D.C.

- **June 7th** - CPI co-sponsored an event on the Peaceful Reunification of Korea at the Los Angeles Family Church, attended by over 100 people.
- **July 22nd** - The CPI book *Kamala Harris & the Future of America* was banned from Amazon for seven days without explanation, coinciding with Kamala Harris becoming the Democratic Party's presumptive nominee. Outrage erupted on social media, leading to 3,000 copies sold in the following days, with CPI highlighted on various YouTube channels.
- **August 19th - 22nd** - During the Democratic National Convention in Chicago, over 1,000 copies of *Kamala Harris & the Future of America* were distributed, along with 1,000 copies of the CPI pamphlet *Do You Believe in Growth?*
- **September 3rd** - CPI members attended the opening of the Uhuru 3 trial in federal court in Tampa, Florida.
- **September 28th** - CPI co-sponsored the Rage Against the War Machine rally in Washington, D.C.

- **October 2nd** - The #PeaceMAGA campaign kicked off at Trump Tower. CPI members unfurled a large banner depicting Donald Trump and Kim Jong Un shaking hands, with the slogan "Only Peace Can Make America Great Again."
- **October 12th** - CPI held a workshop titled "Working Families First!" in the Chicago area.
- **October 27th** - The CPI #PeaceMAGA initiative attended Trump's rally at Madison Square Garden. The banner was noticed and featured by *New Yorker* magazine.
- **October 30th** - CPI member Penny Arcos confronted Congresswoman Ilhan Omar in Minnesota, shouting, "No Money for Rich Men's Wars!"
- **November 2nd** - CPI participated in the "Black is Back" march to support the Uhuru 3 in Washington, D.C.

2023 Timeline of CPI Activities

- **February 19th** - CPI sponsored the largest anti-war rally in Washington, D.C. since 2008, the Rage Against the War Machine rally, alongside the Libertarian Party and the People's Party. CPI later hosted a reception for Scott Ritter, attended by 200 people.
- **March 5th** - CPI published the groundbreaking book *Where Is America Going? Marxism, MAGA, and the Coming Revolution*. The book was translated into Chinese and featured in *Global Times* and on *The Kim Iversen Show*.
- **March 25th - 26th** - CPI held a two-day conference in Washington, D.C. called "The Summit Against Hypocrisy" to counter Joe Biden's "Summit for Democracy." The event featured speeches from numerous prominent guests, and Peter Coffin produced a documentary based on the event.
- **March 30th** - In New York City, CPI members confronted the President of Taiwan outside her hotel, shouting, "Stop selling war in our country! China is not our enemy!"

- **May 29th** - CPI participated in the New York City Peace March, alongside prominent ministers, rabbis, and imams. CPI held its own rally in Union Square with Rage Against the War Machine allies, followed by a march to the United Nations.
- **June** - CPI held a three-day weekend workshop in Missouri to bring members together, welcome new members, and unify the organization.
- **July 10th** - CPI hosted an event in New York City titled "Money and American Injustice: How the Legal System Targets the Poor." The event highlighted the Uhuru case, and Peter Coffin created a film based on it.
- **August 6th** - CPI sponsored and participated in "Humanity for Peace" rallies across the country. In Portland and Chicago, CPI was the primary organizer, while in New York City, they brought a large contingent to this mobilization marking the anniversary of Hiroshima and raising awareness about the dangers of nuclear war.

- **August 27th** - CPI published *Letter to Bob Avakian*, exposing how the U.S. deep state used the Revolutionary Communist Party to threaten Jimmy Carter and how the organization functioned as an asset of French intelligence for many decades.
- **September 20th** - CPI founder Caleb Maupin interviewed the President of the Islamic Republic of Iran, Ebrahim Raisi, at the United Nations.
- **October** - Amid growing protests in support of Palestine across the country, CPI members joined these mobilizations, emphasizing a populist anti-imperialist message as well as the Uhuru case.
- **October 25th** - The Center for Political Innovation was selected by the Russian Foreign Ministry to lead the U.S. delegation to the 2024 World Youth Festival in Sochi, Russia.
- **November 30th** - CPI members staged small protests at three different campuses across Portland, Oregon.
- **December 1st** - An event supporting the World Anti-Imperialist Platform was held in Portland, Oregon.

- **December 2nd** - CPI held its first national convention, with 160 people gathering in Portland, Oregon, for an anti-imperialist gathering.
- **December 8th - 10th** - A three-day workshop was held in Portland, Oregon, for new members who joined the organization as a result of convention outreach.

Made in the USA
Columbia, SC
11 December 2024

49019025R00065